Singing Crickets

Linda Glaser

ILLUSTRATIONS BY Tess Feltes

M Millbrook Press • Minneapolis

To my mother, Eleanor Glaser—a lover of all animals, including crickets—who kept suggesting I write about crickets and wouldn't give up. Thank you! —L.G.

To my parents, who nurtured a sense of wonder —T.F.

The publisher wishes to thank scientific consultant Richard M. Houseman, Ph.D., Department of Entomology, University of Missouri

Text copyright © 2009 by Linda Glaser
Illustrations copyright © 2009 by Lerner Publishing Group, Inc.

All rights reserved. International copyright secured. No part of this book may be reproduced, stored in a retrieval system, or transmitted in any form or by any means—electronic, mechanical, photocopying, recording, or otherwise—without the prior written permission of Lerner Publishing Group, Inc., except for the inclusion of brief quotations in an acknowledged review.

Millbrook Press
A division of Lerner Publishing Group, Inc.
241 First Avenue North
Minneapolis, MN 55401 U.S.A.

Website address: www.lernerbooks.com

Library of Congress Cataloging-in-Publication Data

Glaser, Linda.
    Singing crickets / by Linda Glaser ; illustrated by Tess Feltes.
        p.   cm.
    ISBN 978–0–8225–8806–1 (lib. bdg : alk. paper)
    1. Crickets—Juvenile literature. I. Feltes, Tess, ill. II. Title.
    QL508.G8G53 2009
    595.7'26—dc22   2008011923

Manufactured in the United States of America
1 2 3 4 5 6 – DP – 14 13 12 11 10 09

Hello, Papa cricket!

How do you sing?
Cricka crick, cricka crick.
You rub, rub, rub
your musical wings.

Cricka crick, cricka crick.
All the papas sing along.
And the mamas all find them
by hearing their song.

Hello, Mama cricket!

How do you hear?
You hear with your knees!
That's where crickets have ears.

Cricka crick, cricka crick.
All the papas sing along.
And the mamas all find them
by hearing their song.

Hello, Mama cricket!

It's time! It's time!
You poke your back end down
and lay egg after egg
safely into the ground.

Then off you go.
Good-bye! Good-bye!

Sleep tight, cricket eggs.
Here you'll all stay
in the cold winter earth
until one warm day. . . .

Hello, baby crickets!

You've hatched. It's spring!
Baby boy crickets,
can you sing? Can you sing?
Not yet. Not yet.
You only have wing buds—
not cricket wings yet.

Can you hop? Can you hop?
Yes! What a hop you've got.
What long back legs!
What strong back legs!
You hop and hop
and HOP, HOP, HOP.

You eat and hop
and hop and eat.
You hop away from hungry ones
that want you for a crunchy treat.

You've grown so much
that your skin feels too tight.
You shed it for a bigger one.
Ahh! Now it feels just right.

Now can you sing?
Not yet. Not yet.
You aren't papa crickets yet.
You still must grow your wings.

You eat and grow
and shed your skin
again and again
and again *and* AGAIN.

Look!
At last, you've grown wings!
And *now* you can sing!

You rub, rub, rub
your musical wings.
Cricka, crick. Cricka, crick.
You sing right along
and fill summer nights
with your own cricket song.

You sing with all the papa crickets
to all the listening mama crickets.
Cricka, crick. Cricka, crick.
You join right in.
Cricka crick, cricka crick.
You sing and you SING.

More about Crickets

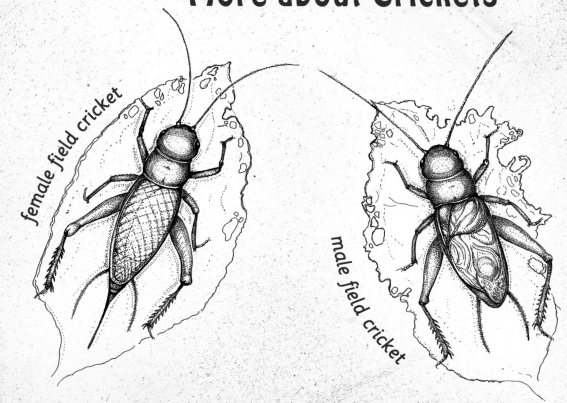

female field cricket

male field cricket

What kind of crickets are pictured in this book? They are field crickets. They're commonly found around the United States in pastures and meadows. The crickets that have "musical wings" are all males because only the males can sing.

How many eggs does a female lay? Each cricket lays between 150 and 400 eggs by poking her needle-shaped back end into the soil.

What makes a cricket's wings "musical"? Male crickets sing or chirp by rubbing their front wings together. Their back wings don't play a part in singing. The males' front wings have a heavy vein with tiny ridges, or teeth. Male crickets lift their wings and rub them together—like a file and scraper. This makes a chirping sound.

Try this: run your fingernail along the teeth of a comb. This is similar to how the cricket's wings make a sound.

Do all cricket songs sound the same? No. Male crickets have at least two songs—a calling song and a courting one. The call is very loud to attract females and to keep other males away. The courting song is much quieter and is done when a female is close by. And each species has its own song. Crickets sing at different rates depending on the temperature. Most sing faster when the temperature is higher.

How do crickets hear with their knees? Crickets don't have actual ears as we do. They do have two eardrums that allow them to hear sounds. While we have eardrums inside of our ears, a cricket's eardrums are below the joint of each front leg. A cricket's eardrum looks like a pale round spot.

What's the difference between crickets and grasshoppers? Crickets are related to grasshoppers. They both have large, jumping hind legs. However, crickets have extremely long antennae—as long as or longer than their bodies. Also, crickets are awake at night while grasshoppers are up during the day.

How high can crickets jump? They can jump as high as 3 feet (0.9 meters) in the air. That's about 20 to 30 times their body length. **Try this:** Measure your height. Multiply that by 20. That's how high you could jump if you were a cricket. For example, if you are 3 feet (0.9 m) tall, you could jump at least 60 feet (18 m) high. That's about the height of a five-story building!

Can crickets fly? Some crickets use their back wings to fly short distances. But crickets mainly move by jumping rather than flying.

How many times does a cricket shed its skin? From the time it hatches to the time it is an adult, a cricket may shed its skin 10 times! The scientific name for the cricket's skin is *exoskeleton*. It is a hard covering that does not stretch. Crickets do not have actual wings until they shed their exoskeleton for the last time.

What do crickets eat? They eat seeds, plants, dead insects, leather, paper, and old cloth—especially wool and silk and other natural materials.

How many types of crickets are there? There are about 900 species around the world.

To hear a cricket sound, visit:
http://www.insecta-inspecta.com/crickets/field/index.html